THE AUTHOR

Penelope J James spent her first twenty-two years living in Cheltenham. In 1969 she married and lived for a short time in South Wales before moving to Norfolk where she lived for many years and where both her son and daughter were born. Later in 1985 she moved to Devon where she now lives with her husband, son and daughter. She has two Bassett hounds and a Burmese cat.

Her hobbies as well as writing poetry and short stories include walking the moors with her two dogs, flower arranging, gardening, sewing and postcard collecting. She is also a member of the Old Plymouth Society and the Thomas Hardy Fellowship.

Pene has drawn on many personal experiences when writing this first collection of verse and hopes that it will give pleasure to those of you who ponder these pages.

Penelope J James is a pseudonym.

1

PENE'S POEMS

by

Penelope J James

Published in England in 2005
By Hatru Books,
34 Powderham Road, Hartley Vale, Plymouth,
Devon.
PL3 5SG.

Design by:
Penelope J James,
34 Powderham Road, Plymouth PL3 5SG

A CIP record of this book is available from the
British Library

ISBN 0-9551207

I wish to dedicate this collection of verse in memory
of Brenda, my mother and my greatest friend.

__ACKNOWLEDGEMENTS__

My thanks are due, imprimis to my husband David, for his tolerance and patience in undertaking to do the typesetting, my son Robin and daughter Jessica for encouraging me to carry on and see my work in print and my three furry friends who lay at my feet through thick and thin. Thank you all for your support.

"Wisdom is the principal thing; therefore get wisdom: and with all thy getting get understanding." Proverbs 4:7

Contents

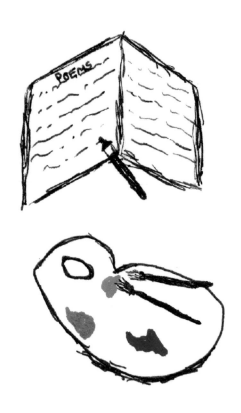

<u>ART IN WORDS</u>

A poet is an artist

His palette full of words

A portrait or a landscape

Animals or birds.

This time a surreal landscape

To which he'll apply his hand

Of distant reaching horizons

Which turn from sea to land.

The land is of the richest red

With buildings made of glass

Where rivers run of purest gold

And deepest purple grows the grass.

Birds cannot fly but only walk

And mountain ranges none can cross

Many an animal has tried

Even the seven toed Albatross.

There's no place for humans here

Rivers of gold are very hot

Man's extinct in this strange place

Animals graze carefully at this spot.

Along the rivers edge

Gold statues of animals stand

Representing those who'd ignored warnings

And lapped the rivers in this land.

Where rivers run hot

And the land is of the richest red

Glasshouses and temples begin to melt

The picture fades; the poet then retires to bed.

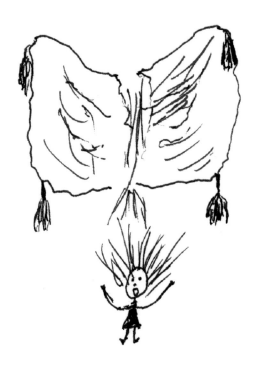

CHOICES

A long marriage is like being
   on a very soft velvet cushion

It folds up around you and makes
   you feel comfortable and safe

It can also come up around you
   just too much and suffocate you

On good days the suffocation
   gives way to the comfortable feeling

Then a sharp quill from one
    of the feathers sticks into you

Making you spring up and away
    from the comfortable position

You are now cast up and away,
    floating and free

The choices are yours whether to
    fall back into safety

Or to go on floating and see where
    it takes you, the choice is yours

The choice is yours.

The prickly feeling fades away
  and you find yourself helplessly

Floating back down onto the soft
  velvet cushion

You have fallen so hard,
  you make a hole in the cushion

Falling down, down, down through the hole,
  into oblivion

Yes, you are free again,
  but the choice is no longer yours

Gravity now determines your path,
  the choice is not yours

The choice has gone.

CHURCH ON A HILL

I climbed to the top of a very steep hill,

To visit a church standing tranquil and still

I entered the church and sat in a pew

And studied a memorial to a family named Drew.

I walked up the aisle the altar to see

Up the steps, one, two, three

Stained glass reflected beautiful lights

From memorial windows at great heights

Glass of red, yellow, green and blue

Shone down on the altar and steps too

As I stood and watched there

The colours fell upon my hair

I looked around me then to see

The church was empty apart from me

And yet I felt a presence there

But there was no-one, no where

I then revisited the pew

Overlooked by the Memorial to Drew

I knelt there for a while and prayed

I can't remember how long I stayed

Until I thought I heard a voice outside

And the door swung open wide

I looked around everything was still

The church remained very tranquil

CLOCKS

"The clocks change today" my mother said

At 2 o'clock when you're tucked up in bed

He wondered if Napoleon's hat with the Westminster chimes

Would turn into a nursery clock playing rhymes.

Would the cuckoo in the clock

Stop cuckooing and instead tick tock

Would the grandfather clock in the hall

Shrink into a grandaughter and become very small.

Waking up, he looked about

He ran downstairs and gave a shout

"Mum, Mum, have the clocks changed, Mum?"

"Why yes, of course, they have son."

"They haven't. The grandfather clock is just as tall

It hasn't shrunk and become very small.

Napoleon's hat with the Westminster chimes

Isn't now playing nursery rhymes."

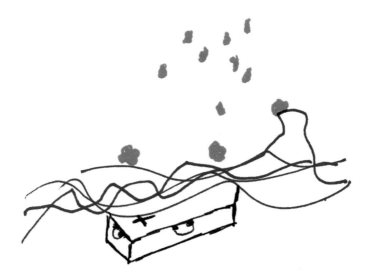

<u>DELIRIUM</u>

A moment in time as you and I

See loves vision like a void in the sky

Winter white music, stormy winds scream

Through the lake like a delirious dream.

Above the cool blue sea shines a diamond moon

Beneath the whispering water lies a deathly tomb

Black shadowy mists, petals red as blood

Watch like a goddess over the flood.

<u>DONKEY DAYS</u>

The days were shorter now

The limbs much stiffer too

The stable and the paddock

Were coming into view.

Oh! good, to have a lie down

At last to rest in straw

To nibble the odd carrot

And then be given more.

The children would be coming soon

Hurrying down the lane

Do I hear their voices calling

Yes, I do. Here comes John and Jane.

The children were at the gate

Offering apples and carrots galore

Jenny brayed and was

Soon out of the stable door.

I so wanted to join in the fun

So I began to get up too

But my limbs were oh! so stiff

I didn't know what to do.

I began to stumble across the paddock

Towards the old wooden stile

Would I ever get there

It felt like walking a mile.

Good, made it at last

John and Jane stroked my ears

Fondled my neck, stroked my back

Looked into my eyes and saw the tears.

"Look, Mum, I think Neddy's ill

And now it's started to rain

You'd better start walking back

Into your stable again."

Back into the dry and the warm

Where he lay down sleeping

He dreamt of the days of his youth

Running, jumping and leaping.

Jenny was always by his side

Walking on the warm wet sand

Listening to the children's laughter

Playing with bucket and spade in hand

The happy voices begging for a ride

"Please Mum let us have a go"

Just one ride, please Mum, please

Once on our backs we'd walk quite slow.

Taking special care so they wouldn't fall

Walking slow to the Punch & Judy stand

Then turning round and going slowly back

Across the wet uneven sand

Reliving his youthful days through dreams

Kept him happy and peaceful in many ways

Jenny looked on, nudged him now and again

And didn't look forward to lonely days.

When John and Jane visit now

And stand to call by the two white gates

Just one lone donkey, Jenny

Ambles from her stable, stands and waits.

DREAM HOUSE

A house appeared in a dream

A house that I had never seen

Night after night I kept on dreaming

Of the same house with no meaning.

The door stood open wide

I looked around and stepped inside

I went down steps, one, two, three

In front of me was a Christmas tree

People singing, laughing and talking

Nobody saw me, I just kept walking

Through an archway into another room

Where between the curtains shone the moon.

The next door took me back outside

Into a garden huge and wide

Everything bright as the moon shone

I looked behind me, the house was gone.

FAT CAT

Mrs So & So was fat

She had an even fatter cat

He was the "apple of her eye"

'til the day he ate the pie

She was not at all impressed

And changed into her Sunday best

Into a basket cat was placed

And with the very greatest haste

Her footsteps got much quicker

Down the road to see the Vicar

"What can I do" he then said

"I don't know just use your head"

He then had a cunning plan

For he was a canny man

"Get him out and hold him tightly

Kneel down and pray to the Almighty"

Cat struggled and broke free

Ran out of church and up a tree

Firemen called to the scene

Saw fat cat in the green

Branches of the tree so high

And eventually by and by

Cat was rescued by a man

A man "who knows a man that can"

A new home was found quite soon

And now he "dances to a different tune"

As the new owner Mrs Lynn

Keeps him oh! so very thin.

FURRY FOUR LEGGED FRIEND

The four fat feet ran over the ground

Stopping to listen to any sound

The long floppy ears listening all the way

Not stopping or wanting to stay.

Just kept going until "What's that smell?"

Her nose told her all was not well

"I'll go and see, I'll soon find out

What that awful smell's about."

"Ah lovely, a decaying bird

The smell's always better than what I heard"

Gobble up quick here and there

"Here girl, here, oh where oh where

Has she got to now

Is that her by that cow?"

Rolling over this way and that

"Oh no", she muttered she's now in a cow pat.

The smell reached her before the dog

She'd ended her walk by jumping in a bog

Walking the moors they loved so well

Mistress and dog on tor and dell

Rides in the car and trips to towns

Visits to friends who lived on "The Downs".

She was there for the tears and smiles as well

Abi listened to the many tales I'd tell

Together always every day

And that's the way they'd always stay

But now there in the heart of the moors

Under a tree below where the kestrel soars

There lies my furry four legged friend

My constant companion to the very end.

<u>GRAVESTONES</u>

There's many a tale to be told

From gravestones so very old

One grave over by the gate

Tells of a particular person's fate.

He was a sailor Oh! so brave

Who ended his days in a watery grave

A memorial stone was placed here

By his widow and friends dear.

His name was Captain Alan Gough

Who sailed the oceans calm and rough

His is a tale that one must tell

For it was in 1890 that the rigging fell

They struggled for many a day

To keep the ship going on it's way

But when the rigging began to fall,

Captain Gough was heard to call

"Abandon ship, Abandon ship"

Then one by one the crew would slip

A life ring around their waist

And then with the greatest haste

Drop down into the oceans deep

The sea their souls to keep

Watery Atlantis is the grave

Of the great seafaring brave.

KEPT IN THE DARK

I'm 18 today, but no presents galore

My mother surprised me with a little bit more

Today on this my 18th Birthday

I learnt of a sister she'd given away.

I left and kept on going down the street

I could hear my mother's running feet

She was calling out to say

"Stop, please, come back and stay".

You are much more than a sister in

You are sister dear my identical twin

Sister, Sister where are you now?

I shall try and find you but I don't know how.

I've always felt not quite whole

My spirit yearning for a lost soul

It may take a month, it may take a year

But I'll never give up sister dear.

LADIES WHO LUNCH

Twin-setted ladies wearing jewellery galore

Came bustling through the hotel door

These ladies had all come to lunch

Large in number and a very mixed bunch.

They chattered and nattered and talked some more

Then a few late-comers walked through the door

Everyone turned their head

No-one listened to what the Chairman said

The members were looking to see who was late

No-one was joining in the debate

Suddenly the Treasurer was saying a word

"A £3 increase in membership" was heard

All eyes and ears were in her direction

This news gave some apoplection!!

Then the members sat down to eat

They ate and drank and were quite replete.

Then a "Speaker" talked about flowers

And of Egyptian art and floral bowers.

The talk then over, the raffle done

Members arose and all begun

To leave the room happy and content

At the end of a day very well spent.

NEW BEGINNINGS

Anticipation, Joy & Hope

These are the contents of the traveller's suitcase

Scenes of future destinations above the seats

Fill the unaccustomed traveller's heart with promise.

Promise of what, escape, holiday, work or pleasure?

Within the traveller's heart lies a spirit for adventure

And the final emergence from the vehicle

Gives a sense of rebirth into an unknown void.

Carefully, take my hand, help me please,

Take care of my suitcase it's contents are unique.

A higher voice speak to me guide me –

I have now taken your hand.

NINETEEN AND GOING NOWHERE

Silver shoes pinching toes

Black fishnet panty hose

Mini skirt above the knee

Look in mirror

Oooo Is that me?

Pearlised pink lipstick

Mascara laid on thick

Back-combed brown hair

Look in mirror

Oooo is that me there?

She crept across the hall

Father then gave a call

"Is that you going out?"

Look in mirror

Oooo now much in doubt.

Father stood there on the mat

"You're not going out dressed like that"

"Oh please my friends will be"

Look in mirror

Upstairs one, two, three.

Off with the shoes pinching toes

Off with the black panty hose

Off with the mini skirt made herself

Look in mirror

Now I know I'm "on the shelf".

ONE WOMAN & HER DOG

Chimneys billowed forth applewood smoke

Into a darkening indigo sky

An old woman in a woolly cloak

Leaning on her stick walked by.

Her little dog wagged his tail

He loved his walks and running free

Her gait was slow, her skin was pale,

Echoing her age was the old oak tree.

Hobo's battle for life now lost

Was more than the woman could bear

She looked out at the morning frost

She'd now no reason left to care.

The old woman's breath rose

Like incense into the cold air

Her life was slowly coming to a close

Her pale face framed by greying hair.

A service was held in a couple of days

In memory of Maggie and her faithful friend

They remembered their many delightful ways

Both together again at the very end.

__PEACE AT LAST__

Was it alive or was it dead?

The body that lay in the bed.

Very cold and oh! so still

Was the body dead or ill?

I stood amazed afraid to touch

This person, whom I loved so much.

"Please move, please wake!"

No response, afraid to give a shake.

A shiver ran along my spine

As I watched this body so supine

I knelt closer and started to pray

Took her hand and heard her say

"Nice of you to visit me here

Get yourself a chair and sit by me dear"

I didn't know whether to laugh or cry

But just stood looking and gave a sigh.

POLITICAL JOURNEY

Once proud to be English and hold your head high

To walk those green pastures beneath a blue sky

To speak proper English to be understood

What of these values, sadly lost now for good.

"Charity begins at home" or so I've been told

Now our lovely small island's left out in the cold

I read in the papers the Governments' given more

To help fund yet another overseas war.

The hospitals housing the sick and dying

Investment offices housing those apt at lying

To the ordinary man with redundancy pay

You'll make a fortune if you invest this way.

So the sick and dying invested their pays

To help them during their illness days

Investments lost what could they do

Join the bottom of an NHS queue.

Buildings the thing now everywhere

Forget the "green belt" just build anywhere

Governments' building 'castles in the air'

But then I ask you "what do they care?"

Backhanders to builders here and there

Luxury flats or future slums "what do they care?"

As long as Governments' and tycoons prosper well

To the man in the street, "What the hell!"

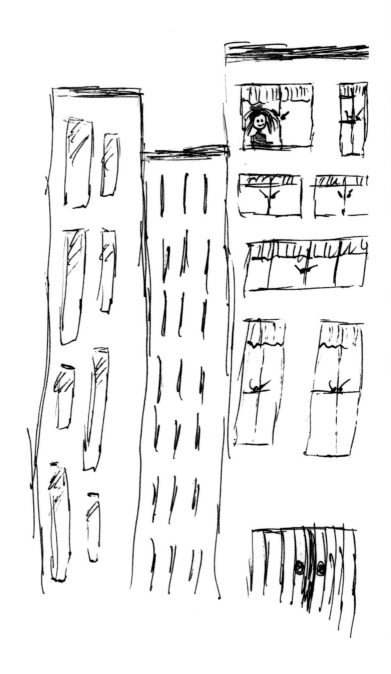

SANDRA LIVES HERE

Red painted nails and cheap perfume

Permeated the air in the sitting room

Dingy and dark, musty and stale

Stains on the carpet from last night's ale.

The needle sticking in the record groove

Sandra slumped in a chair, unable to move

Married again with a different surname

Many years since and the scene is the same

With red painted nails and cheap perfume

Sandra smoked pot in the dingy room

Forty floors up and ever so high

The view from the window was only the sky

She drew deeply on her cigarette

And tried to remember when she'd last ate.

Was it yesterday or the day before?

She couldn't remember it may have been more.

When had her life like this begun?

Probably with the birth of her son

She wondered about his life, what he'd done

Sixties ended sadly but at first they'd been fun.

How her arm and shoulder hurt

She hadn't meant to upset Kurt

But time and time again

She'd always seemed to upset men.

Sandra's looks were now very faded

She'd lost vitality and her charisma jaded

She'd longed for a garden and house of her own

A place she'd be proud of to call her home

She slumped down in the old armchair

And felt overcome with deep despair

Just one more shot in the arm

Just one more, what's the harm?

Red painted nails and cheap perfume

The air of drugs and death filled the room

She ended her days all alone

In rented rooms, not a home of her own.

"SARAH-LOU" HAIRDRESSERS

Short, tall, fat and thin

All the ladies walked in

To a room hot and steamy

First lady was Mrs Heaney

"A perm, blow dry or set?"

"A blow dry today, thank you pet".

Then Mrs Heaney's sharp tongue

Began to wag and one by one

Others heard her harsh remarks

"What's that you say about Mrs Sparks?"

Asked the kindly Mrs Fraye,

"You want to watch, just what you say,

Mrs Sparks is my best friend

You want to start to mend

Your gossipy and wilful tongue

It'll end in trouble before day's done"

Then once Mrs Pugh joined in

The Hairdressers became an awful din.

Mesdames, Heaney, Fraye and Pugh

Started throwing combs and brushes too

One brush caught Sally on the chin

"Stop it, stop it, stop this din!"

The owner Mrs Hairum shouted

Then another flying brush clouted

Mrs Hairum on the rear

Will you listen, hear! hear!

Then a gruff voice was heard say

"I was just passing this way"

There stood policeman PC Brown

Looking stern with a fearsome frown

Then he ducked a flying brush

He shouted "Hush, There must be hush,

That's enough, this must end"

Then he called his policeman friend

P.C. Scareum, who then stated

"It's time all this din's abated

Do you want to spend a night in jail?"

Silence reigned and all turned pale

And that's why Heaney, Fraye & Pugh

Are banned from hairdresser's "Sarah-Lou".

SPELLBOUND

Whizz, bang, wallop what was that?

A muffled meow; there stood a frog instead of a cat

The witch looked around somewhat bemused

Another spell wrong, she felt most confused.

One more go, she'd not give in

Tail of mouse and a fish's fin

Some tinctures of green, of blue and red

She tried to remember what the spell book said

With spectacles lost and no book to hand

She was just beginning to understand

Why her potions and lotions were all going wrong

Of course, she'd forgotten to sing the song

"Newt, fish, frog and lizard wave my wand

All caught from the meadow pond

Squirrel, bat and bird make three

All caught from the Rowan tree

Stir the potion thrice times round

Swirl about and fall to the ground

Reach up high and stretch down low

Now the potion's ready to go."

What's happened to me the cat was shrieking

Change me back I'm tired of leaping

"I'm doing my best; just wait a tick

I've lost my wand I'll use this stick"

She waved the stick this way and that

The frog remained, no sign of the cat.

Oh dear, what am I doing wrong

I chanted the spell and sung the song.

When all of a sudden from across the room

Came running and shrieking the witch's broom.

"You've not used me, that's what's wrong

You have to fly on me, and sing the song."

So on the broom ever so high

The witch sang the song from up in the sky

The broom gave a piercing laugh and shriek

"You think I like flying for you everyday of the week"

It tossed her off and down she fell

And landed in a disused well

Next she heard a gurgled cry

Then she saw the frog close by

"Well fancy seeing you down here"

He laughed and gave an evil sneer

The witch said "It's OK for you"

Then she sneezed Atishoo, Atishoo, Atishoo

Three sneezes changed him to a cat

Floundering around where she sat

On a ledge half way down the well

And that is where they both still dwell.

SPRINGTIME

For many months the trees lay bare

Plants hidden underground trying to survive

Through the long cold winter months

Before leaves and plants start to arrive.

Flying through skies changing from grey to blue

Birds are busy building nests on the wing

Looking down from trees changing from brown to green

Making a home for their young, birds begin to sing.

Cows now let out from winter stabling to graze

Munch the luscious green grass in place of hay

Looking about they observe the scent of fresh air

And walk their new pastures and fields of yesterday.

The fox exits his den and looks about

The smells of gorse and heather are carried in the air

As well as mice, stoats and weasels

His nostrils twitch, his dinner is everywhere.

STATE OF AFFAIRS

Winds blew, rivers rose

Sun drenched skin hung on skeletal frames

Frames, frames, frames

Just people, none bore names

Get out, don't come back,

Children with no place to hide

Hide, hide, hide

Poverty left no room for pride

The colour of your skin

Whether you are black or white

White, white, white

Who says what is right?

Religion brings people together

Religion creates war

War, war, war,

I wonder who's right; what's more?

Education, the old and frail

Homeless, the sick and dying

Dying, dying, dying

Who care's? Even the Government's lying.

THE DIET

Today is the day

That I must weigh

I just can't believe my eyes

I've actually dropped a size

This diet's paying off

I really mustn't go and scoff

Doughnuts with too much jam

I must now stick to having

Plenty of salad and ham

The weight keeps coming off

But how I really want to scoff

Chocolate, liquorice and mints galore

Sugared almonds, toffees and very much more.

THE HUNT

Four and forty men set out to kill

The morning air was frosty and chill

Four and forty horses waiting for the horn

The hunt was off on this February morn.

Four and forty hounds waiting for the chase

The leader of the pack setting the pace

Eight and eighty animals, four and forty men

To chase one fox right into his den.

The fox watched from Vixen Tor

He could see them coming across the moor

He'd lost his own mother in this way

He knew he had to run, he could not stay.

Through brambles, mud, water and fern

His ageing frame felt his feet burn

His heart racing faster and faster still

Above all the noise the horn so shrill.

Memories kept on coming back

As he ran past the old wooden shack

That was where his mother died

He remembered how he'd cried and cried.

He remembered his brothers and sister watched on

And then there was this man with a gun

"Kinder to shoot them, they've no mother now"

Humans called this kind, he couldn't see how.

"Oh no!" they were closing in on him fast

Den's not too far now, "Oh! home at last"

But eight and eighty animals, four and forty men

Set about destroying the poor old fox's den.

Men began to dig and others came and helped

The hounds now had him how he cried and yelped.

His son watched from Vixen Tor

At the mayhem below on the moor.

He remembered clearly his mother said

"Son do you know why their coats are red?

Because they don't want our blood to show

They don't want other outsiders to know".

"Not all humans are the same

There are those that go by a different name

They're called the anti-hunt brigade

They fight for us, they are not afraid."

"We have to hope they win the day

So foxes can roam the moors and stay

Otherwise my darling son

They'll have us before the day is done".

THE NUN

Sister Bernadette walked slowly down the stairs

Holding the bannister to steady her weak frame

She shivered in the chill night air

And hoped her face denied her pain.

She knelt and bent her head to pray

Her knarled fingers grasped the altar rail

"Why was my life directed in this way?"

She looked at her hands they were awfully pale.

Seventy years she had lived this life

Serving the Lord by helping others

Giving up the chance to become a wife

Or that of becoming a mother.

She heard footsteps walking up the nave

She finished praying and turned to look

Sister Bridget whispered "I know you're being brave

Let us read together from the Holy Book".

THE OLD MAN

The door creaked open wide,

I looked around and crept inside.

The room was like a hoarders refuge

Paintings and a stuffed bear so huge.

I opened a box a tune started to play

From deep in the room I heard a voice say

"Come on in child don't be afraid

I wish to talk with you" so I stayed.

We talked for hours the old man and I

Tales of war and how he lost his eye.

"Did you like the box that played the tune?

You can have it; but come again soon".

So I did I went every day

We'd sit and talk and listen to him say

"I remember when I was about your age

I dreamt of being an actor of going on stage"

"Why didn't you then?" "Because of the war

Dreams of all kinds were to be no more"

"So you go follow your dreams son

Follow those dreams go and have fun".

I miss the old man now he's passed away

I lift the music box lid and listen to it play.

Memories flood back of the man so old

And of the many stories so often told.

THE PARK

The wind blew harshly around her face

Her gloved hands still felt very chill

The park today seemed a hostile place

Her footsteps slow as she walked uphill.

Lost in thought, not looking around

She walked at a very slow pace

Her steady gait over uneven ground

Onwards she went to her resting place.

She sat on the seat as so oft before

Scattered bread for the birds to eat

She then threw down a little more

Birds now feeding by her feet.

She felt tired and weary of it all

The church bell chimed loud and clear

She endeavoured to rise but had a fall

Muttered to herself "oh dear, oh dear!"

She knew it was her final walk

She struggled home and into bed

Then she heard the doctor talk

She didn't like what he said.

"You can't stay here on your own

There is no one to care for you

You must go into a nursing home

That is what you must do."

With this she gave a scream

"I must, must I" she cried

This is like a bad dream

And with that she died.

THREE FRIENDS FOR TEA

Two Jeans and Pene met for tea

They were good friends these three

In February at Pene's they met

The table with biscuits and tea was set

They nattered and chattered and chattered and nattered

Pene upset the table and everything clattered

Down to the floor in an awful heap

Waking the dogs that had fallen asleep

Now I know why they say "let sleeping dogs lie"

For all of a sudden the dogs gave a cry

Of pure delight as they ate up the food

Now the three were in a sombre mood

No biscuits, cake, coffee or tea

Were left on the table for these three

"Don't worry now, come with me

I've something to show you come and see"

Pene led the way to another room

There a music box played a tune

They stood and listened to it play

Then the two Jeans were heard to say

"Look at the time, it's time we went

We've really enjoyed the morning we've spent

Nattering and chatting and talking some more

"Bye, Bye" – silence fell as she closed the door.

VISITORS

The old man rose from the rustic seat

Put down his mug and plate

Walked down the path to meet

Two strangers standing by the gate.

"Hello there", he said as he walked

"Who are you? Speak I cannot see"

The strangers greeted him and talked

"Now please come in, join us for tea.

A woman came out and greeted them too

"I'm Polly and this is Joe"

"Dad likes to talk to people like you

And misses the company when you go"

With promises that they'd call again,

The old man, waited day by day,

Voices were heard that sounded the same

"Here we are, we were passing this way".

They talked of the war

Of his time in the Far East

His awful experiences and more

Then Gwen entered with a teatime feast.

"Tell me child, what colour is your hair?

Are your eyes dark or the palest blue?

Is your hair dark or fair?

Describe your eyes in the fairest hue."

"My hair is really very fair

My eyes are of the deepest blue

Give me your hand to touch my hair

Outline my face and eyes too."

"You are so kind to a frail old man

Whose light and dark remain the same

Tell me a little now of your young man

Remind me also of his name."

"My name is Joseph but I'm called Joe"

"Well I never my name's the same

Tell me you're not in a hurry to go

I'm really so glad that you both came."

He spoke of his life as an engineer

Showed them various things he'd made

"You see, once I could see quite clear

But being elderly my sight began to fade.

Gwen and her father stood at the gate,

The young couple left hand in hand

It was now, dusk and getting late

Gwen likened her life to drifting sand.

Gwen and her father went indoors

"It's awfully cold, going to be a frost"

She thought of Clay and many more

And of the different loves she'd lost.

Her mother's voice still rang clear

"I don't like ringing you at work Gwen

But your father's had a stroke my dear,

When can you return home then?"

Home she'd been ever since, when?

She couldn't remember the exact date

On reflection she realised then

Her life's journey was getting late.

She thought of happy days with "Clay"

Walks together along the sands

Stopping for kisses on the way

Walking along happily holding hands.

How different life might have been

Had she not returned home to stay

She reflected and began to dream

Finally stooping down to pray.

WATERY LANDSCAPE

Where rocks meet the sea

And the wind blows free

Seagulls call from on high

From an azure blue sky.

White sea horses race

At a quickening pace,

Sun and clouds move past,

Long dark shadows are cast.

As the tide is now low

More sand begins to show,

Seas secrets now lie bare

Rock pools exposed here and there.

Adults walk hand in hand

Children play in the sand

Small rock pool creatures hide

As nets are cast wide.

If you enjoyed this book, you may like to read the second collection of Pene's Poems to be published in the autumn of 2006.